Table of content:

Foreword

Honestly, I haven't the slightest idea what to write here. A bit of data about me, I suppose. Well: My name is Raducanu Alexandru – George (no one calls me like that, never used that name), born on 10th of December 1994, in Bucharest. I've started this volume of lyrics a while ago, in a pretty foggy period of my life, where I could not tell apart this thing from that thing, and then I dropped it, because life decided it was time to throw in my path new challenges. Now, why should you read my aberations?

Well, firstly because reading is beneficial to the brain (scientifically proved, not by me), secondly because it is completely possible fo you to like what you are reading, even though you will not make any sense of it. And you don't have to. And lastly (hopefully), in the event of you finding yourself in these lyrics, and you give them your own meaning, I hope they will help you go through whatever it is you are going through right now. That's about it.

Enjoy reading it.

Heart, resonate, with the beats of the planet, with billions of other hearts, and the mysteries of the universe shall be understood.

Epic

I see red moons from the tide, I see thoughts mirrored in the wind.

They swing...

With my thought, with puppet strings,

Like, when a rock is binding you,

And you fall with it in oceans of ideas, of everything, of nothing.

Listen, your water is ringing...

Take it. Put it in a closet and tie it.

With a string of focalized, saved light.

Tie it to the padlock.

Dark – like

Wind howls in my mind,

Ideas hanging in my phone,

I have... dearchived thoughts,

And darkend be my eyes, they close.

In epic genre, colors break in blue vinyls,

Modules, arias, sparks divided.

Shallow values of density,

And the gates are closing...

Selane, selane the breeze wails,

When you, enter the sea.

Too deep, too... painful.

        the voice..........

            The voice..........

                The Voice .

Introduction

Various domains, various pens,

Various phones.

You're trading phones for an aquarium.

You give a penny for a fish, and two for those interested.

You place the aquarium to the fish, you tie it to it's snout.

I'm asking you, he's asking you, they all, yourself,

Themselvs, are asking...

Is it?

They come back from bed, they complain on a chair...

Keys are placed in frogs, and they go: groac-groac, Groac-Groac.

Cable

Wires. . . cables . . .

Twisted, coiled, rainbow wires, idea wires

Glimpse through the light.

I see them dancing to the rhythms of the modern waltz.

I've got enough smoking three-stranded skates or

Wires or. . . . .whatever, you put them in the sun,

you lather 'em up, you let 'em put sleep around your eyelashes,

And you fall asleep, floating in blue rivers.

Est votum demonstrandum

My face is popping from too much stillness.

Colours are seen, balconies are broken,

Ideological atoms speak the song of the fog.

Mechanized titans complexify contemplating homonymy

From the circuit.

The voltage has frozen. I see you!

But it's not you... you're sliced with meticulousness

By a grotesque centipede, like a snake that calligraphs

With unassailable white ink.

They drag you in chains, on the land cleared of weeds

Where my depressions say:

It will rain.

vascularized opening

What needs to secure,

What do you unravel from a flood of self-realizations?

How can you abstract a light bulb,

Whose filament climbs steadily towards a sputtering light?

When you discover what lurks on the wings of fear,

You shudder, and see your thoughts scattered,

distorted, full of objective miasmas.

You climb with hope, aspiring to something high...

You stop and gesticulate to the darkness

On the other side of you.

Something of the kind that completes the fact that you exist.

Up you look, slam the door in my face.

Scared, you open your eyes:

What do you see?

The Correct dosage

I have exhausted all my efforts,

I'm training myself to overcome the upgrade on the outside.

I decide I'll slam the TV to the ceiling-lamp.

But, I can't. . ...it's already hanging there, and I...

I'm in a balanced external conflict.

I can't figure out why fantasies are dripping from the chandelier.

I check the TV, it's plugged in.

Ugh,

I don't have qualitative ideas like him

He wants to put concentrated morphine in his bloodstream;

It doesn't work, he wants us, he can't.

He doesn't have the right dosage.

Distorted pressures

With a style of humanity befitting the twenty-first century,

We complain, we comment, we choke on the arrogance we give ourselves.

Forlorn, desolate. . ...like the city you are same.

And with an overwhelming amazement

You reflect yourself in the mirror. You're reaching for a new era

Of defeated idealism. . .

Can you resend the psychoanalysis,

Next to expired collagen?

Or how to feel your degreased brain

Vaporized and denominated?

You're so alarmed,

Like a cycle of evanescent gravel muck.

is the same thing...

Go, adjust your brain pressure.

I am not lonely

I'm always, always trying to find keys, bracelets and lots of veils,

that because of the clause I make a hunch

and I hit bottomless water.

In fact, it becomes an empty waterfall

Out of which I fish swirling chills and from which I bring spirals of light.

From whence they come again and again, a bit lonely. and the movement,

his gesture and posture, make me think

I have hope.

I go to other diversified domains,

consuming my fuel, consuming my efforts.

I see a flicker:

I go towards it and

It's not lonely, it's naked.

Ultrafiltered phenomenon

Sensational waves bend towards me and I was thinking:

Where do I go to consider the impossible?

What shall I do from everlasting, what shall I light in the net of stars?

Something more than a quantum impression

more than an idealistic boulder,

especially and most especially a mundane gathering of brethren.

The gun aim snapped,

the pack is gathering,

we start rummaging through empty bottles.

Foggy bracelets

Why are clocks visible in the fog?

How they appear, how they disappear. How they are and how I can write,

That's how I can see through the fog.

My hand moves tremblingly forward

it doesn't know what's in front of it. that it's foggy and I touch a bronze statuette.

It's a griffin, eroded by the stale weather.

And it moves, and it catches my hand in its mouth.

It's warm in there.

I can't move it, it's shackled.

It's cold outside. It's foggy, I can't breathe.

I've had fear,

now...

I'm calm. It's foggy.

con fi guration

Oriental harmonies surround me, and

binds me with golden marshmallow thread.

You swing with everything, with nothing

Like a jubilant willow beaten by a wind of candles.

You're happy, you're confused.

You are yourself, and you wonder not so confused:

Why is the world so welcoming?

you reach out to everyone, gathering

crowds of copious ideas.

You seal them in a snug jar, and you lock them up.

And throw it at me.

Targeted by basilisk

For centuries whole and shrunken, we have remained

With two, and a few more programs.

And I shove them, and I shove them in the water

And I think I predominate in the sunset.

Now I represent an ideal in life, that of the woman with a moustache.

And down the stairs again,

I look to other planes of human expansion.

I go to the library, the pawns have moved.

They weren't supposed to, but I like chess paper.

I play.

I'm the rook and take the knight, then,

Checkmate, basilik.

The Sad Puppeteer

With riveted aluminum strings, all will be well.

You're fishing botherings again in bottomless waters. . .

Smells like tears

It smells like sand soaked with bookcover smell,

Smells like a porcelain doll with a cork,

It smells like sore eyes, and I want to reset it.

I repeat none of the normalities, when I cross the valley.

I cross and the train comes: The doll stays on the tracks, denied its fate.

The train shatters all suffering.

It's insulted. . . It's shattered, the doll's dream is shattered.

I see, and I want to retire quietly, to tattoo with the train on the back of my head in the mirror.

No more smelling of broken bottles, no more falling from puppet strings

Undigested flaws.

I've been wandering around.

I was splitting headaches all around me, and the doll,

I'd reach the end of the string.

When it was over,

He'd come back, and we'd get our heads together.

How I look with headphones

From the lake stretched out by the wall, from foggy spectres

The blues rise on a jacket.

A snail on a percussion leaf.

A new hope rising with sleeping thought

And hope that will find the lifeguard lifted by the water

Of the desk drawer's sea.

From the pile of walnut jelly-lined

Even a mummified snail has more talent

You spin in place like a drugged gyroscope,

and you wonder, what the fuck do you want out of life?

In the park

I want to hang myself in the closet

Let my memories flow into the void, and put them against the wall

I hang them on the hanger, but they don't know how to swing

I search my thoughts on the Internet,

but it's fallen from the depths of great distance.

A lucky star comes and in your wet lavender hair,

opens the closet.

The park appears, and the memory bank.

The bench where we got lost last year on a May evening

Or was it two years ago?

You appear,

I appear transparently.

You disappear,

I disappear.

Once upon a time

A someone, a whispering object,

Slowly sending alarm signals

Press on the tea supply and you'll see

what a reception of wax, of paraffin, of candles put

in candlesticks hanging in the pit.

Like the smoke of incense, like the dripping mist that lifts

Towards the edges, dreams that keep falling,

and again they rise, and once more the sea tries.

And the moon rises and rises from the earth.

Once upon a time there was a great moon, and she was.

In the sky

A glimmer of intelligence

I lean on the vault of heaven like a weary man

Of so many elevations.

Some with big rosettes, some with no money, some with nothing coming from the sides...

I've gone sour and I'm thirsty.

And I have no water. I don't have any more mulberry leaves in Cluj because they've been sold.

It's a good thing it's raining, otherwise...

I think I'm drowning in thirst.

A cuckoo appears from a wristwatch.

And the seal, I take the seal by the paw and carry it to the water.

A stone spring slaps me in the face.

It's no use. . .

A wave of silence

I cried a lot, and I washed my tears away in a lake.

I feel my mind exploding, and every time

When I want to burn its fuse I sink into its soothing

wave.

It's full of me all over.

And from my disintegrating veins, I've only a drop left.

What shall I do with it? Throw it away?

Maybe I don't need it anymore but I'll calm myself

When I drink from my puddle

Slowly, slowly, slowly I feel there's a part of you in it.

It's hard for me to destroy you, and your mind won't leave me nor

the camera.

Nor the memory of my phone,

nor my mind emptied of passion.

I destroy myself and rebuild myself over and over again, never

I'm not tired of the windy words.

I want clear, concrete facts, so

so you can start forgetting yourself.

Pains of a violin

When you look at the clock, you see the hour gone and

You look up to re-enter reality.

You struggle to survive. There's great voltage, and

The electric currents, fall to the burning poles and

Falls the history of your drunken knowledge.

You dodge, you run with snail's steps

You see how the blue plasma bursts

burst from pages of cloth.

You look around, you smell the calico and it hurts.

And with a married melody, you watch

At the visions and hallucinations that appear on the screen.

You grab the smoke at the other end of the pole

Then you pick up your violin and start to play

Song of sorrow woven with song of joy.

Too much

I don't know why this is happening.

Why, how, and in what way, but I have no idea

How to make you feel better, how to make you smile?

How does an atom radiate where it is?

Quiet waves of sweet, pleasant poison

like a chocolate damf.

I'd like a lot but... You choose.

You fade, you fade a little bit every day and you know

Too much is bad.

Too much cold, even more than any fear.

From any universe, from whatever you want, if you're there,

Try freedom.

Unanswered questions

Why?

Probably because of that or the other...

Or perhaps I lament, deprecate, desolate drapery...

It's torn, eaten by moths. And they're hungry for imagination.

Why?

That's why! Right?

But which one?!

Make up your mind, woman!

I don't know if I'm tormenting you, or if you're tormenting yourself.

To ignore me completely.

You're telling me to pay attention to the class.

What class? The one where you start wondering again

Why do you ask?

Because that's why you don't want to have anything,

that that something makes you dizzy and quick to

dream about it over and over again.

You suffer.

Why?

I don't know, but I know you don't know either.

I'm haunting through the house's chasm

I'm feeling dizzy

a blur of falling in replay, filmed with a slow-motion camera that defies thermodynamics,

And the fading trickle of blood rising up my forehead

I'm strengthening my conviction that

I'm stuck here in nothingness, and I think I feel a presence giving me

Chills, hovering around me and I'm an oboe player...

I play the oboe with the bow of my trumpet.

The piano swears at me from the parlor at full volume.

I'm afraid of this aromatic haze, it's taking my sleep away.

I turn on my imagination, I fall upwards, in deep silence

It begins to haunt me

The imagination of the abyss in the house.

Only what comes to mind

I slam to the ceiling the feeling of being first and

I hate it when I see hypocritical people.

If you ask them for advice, they'd better let it go.

Maybe it's just my reptilian imagination,

that puts my hands in a jam, and I laugh.

that later I might fall through the grass,

and underwater among the gelatinous amphibians.

I'm slipping

      I look

          I sniff.

It smells like lost love when I sniff again,

And my nose goes ahead of me along the columns of time.

Tarnished, I observe, you wonder at what I say.

But you don't know I'm asleep.

Measuring intensity

Too large

Too good for me, besides

That I deserve something better, more consistent.

Falling down into the green abyss

On a soft, blond lake that is

Slowly dripping down my cheeks.

Salty dew sprinkles that have no purpose

I don't feel like it, because I want a lot and nothing.

more than rest and green eyes,

I measure no more than their intensity,

with the butterflies in my stomach.

From the depths of melody

very loudly beats in my head, and

very softly my heart is dripping

It's already afternoon, what can I do?

The bank is closed.

I've locked it in a wall of enameled terracotta.

It's a bloody sunset and seen from underwater,

It looks like a continuous stream of remote-controlled metal bugs.

Little bubbles of air come out my nostrils, green from...

what have you done?

You were there, you saw that you knew all along

It's a trap.

But I was the bait,

      the target was already caught, twisted.

a discoloured prism.

Flames

it's hot...

it's hot all around me.

I'm boiling like a volcano,

I wish I was a volcano, I'd love to be.

I could blow up streams of lava thoughts

cause I've got too much of that; and

clouds of stinging words,

and ashes, ashes of a burnt soul

by the venom of an invidious flame.

Because of the anger that burns in me,

I have become an entity of fire itself,

and I rage to heights of anger and wrath

and I weep, and acid tears fall to the ground.

I wish I could stop my eruptions of rage

Help me, rain on me

So that instead of papery lava I may end up

Like a mayflower

full of crystallized dew.

From a spray

I sit at my desk...

I sit at my desk gnawed on the inside and I watch

At the phone charger.

Beside me thrones a long-aged blank wall

And full of peasant grime...

I have a full trash can next to me

With my fatal results

of my sitting in my chair at my desk.

I've grown roots from unchewed gum wrappers

and from empty cola bottles, countless gutted ideas

and many thoughts derived

from the darkness of my big bedroom...

they burn, they burn out, they rekindle

they split in two, in threes, in fours, in...

besides

All perish, and are reborn again

They turn into the same or something else, when sunset meets the sea,

The morning stars sing of the humor of the feathery current that lures the leaves.

Something else, nothing. just white.

It's white and all and all again perish.

From above, from the top of the screen, rumbling as a twisted water, slowly descends

To my page. Where but a spot on my skin

Nothing fades

Only something else.

Rainy night

I'm an unripe seed.

Your rain of words no longer falls on me

And my head aches as if it would.

It would explode from the pain...

You may ask, why?!

But you don't want to know since you've taken away

The sap that soothes my mummified soul.

I'm like a sun that's gone out and

You sunk it in your waters, to whom

you took the last drop of essence from it.

I wish I could take my revenge on you in the sweetest way possible

I wish you could feel what it's like to live

A bad dream of unrequited love

On a rainy night

Of May's spring.

How long I've waited

I'm slowly dripping on the cupboard, dripping strands of hair

Wedding threads and ribbons, christening ribbons, they twist, they bend, they wail.

I wonder if you want yourself, accept yourself as you are.

Like a master of grief, a scholar full of foul intellect

At peace with the fact that you exist in this pitiful form,

beneath layers of smoky candlesticks, beneath pieces of chalk

soaked with ink, I wait...

to believe and it still wouldn't be enough to be skeptical

or maybe instead of a brain you have a hard drive, maybe instead

of thoughts, you have chaos of words, circuits.

And you're waiting for Santa Claus to come and bang Christmas on your head...

To clear your head

That you...

You're worse than a peeling wallpaper

From a movie.

Longings

with a riddle of completing thoughts

a tumult of duck-blinds meets me and,

though I do not perceive this poetic context,

I begin to wish for light...

and a cloud of dozing beats in my head, a bell echoes in the deep ocean.

and in your eyes I see alabaster, and I think...

the ocean doesn't have enough pearls

to grant your wish.

You take them, you put them in an album

you try to see your wish, where you are...

And see how on a moonlit night full of colored monkeys

(At the circus),

A smile, on the lips, flies smooth in the night like a quail

Filled with longing

I was walking through snow

it turns out that not every tie of basil

is green.

the sky is green and basil floats on the table.

for many a cup of fallen snow

over my cold mind and frozen

for a long unfinished time,

because you ask:

why don't you feel like making Andalusian wood pellets,

where horses run in flames of sunset?

What's wrong with it? Don't you know that greed eats away at your footsteps

on the blue cloth snow with stingy shyness?

It's cold, the snow blinds my eyes, atrophied by too much blinded fatality.

you pray for many, you huddle in everything, you enjoy this blue snow.

it's warmer, it's airy, it's been around for a long time

under my heart, in my place

completely secret for all to see.

you look up, a pillar; it's long been there, but

you haven't seen through the snow, and

like a proper respectable man, you begin to think

and say to yourself:

We're beating the wind, it's the evening of snow.

you don't know

you're in the dark.

the silence is collapsing over you,

you feel your very soul is burnt,

and you try to understand the lines of implosion.

you feel crushed by what's in your mind, yet you still have enough clarity left

to realize that you did it: you turned off the light

and the darkness is generous, darkness doesn't exist

there is only the absence of light...

and yet it exists: it's behind your skin, it's under your feet,

it's everywhere because you let it

to gnaw at you like a worm, and you can't,

you just can't.

You keep falling, you keep falling, and your thoughts are scattered like bees under the smoke.

You're trying to...

The brightest light makes the darkest dark.

But,

love lights the stars.

Irony

Among astral bells, water comes

Amidst pillars of classical genius the world passes...

Longing for life, longing, and my eyes jump

through my star-filled head.

Seems to ache, seems like veins and arteries and mortars

jump in the sun.

Why does the on purpouseness entwined with the rythm

of life leaves, that suddenly comes to you from somewhere else

Is it leaving?

Madness of alfalfa, hearts hanging in the sky...

Of all the diggings, only mine

they die...

Departures

When I think of some often,

of others coming and going and going,

Then out of the green lightning they come to me

Growing, and how I grow with them.

I see. I hear the shapes go, they scatter

into the world. and in waxed letters, on the slate

I see them. As they sit, drinking their coffee,

discussing my thoughts of spreadness

I bring, by the house I sleep up,

I turn aside to see my plumage,

And of some, only others are gone.

Transposition

a little scourge, a poor shadow of what I once was,

I'm spinning around my tail, blinded by the prospect of reality.

I'm searching, I'm seeing myself. I think. Is it me?

Do I look that frozen?

Is this me? My furiously euphoric self?

Get me out of here, there's no way.

How, no, I'm still a scourge. It's just that...

I'm self-flagellating with perverse thoughts, I'm holding them by the tail so they won't leave

Though it pains me, I love this chaos.

In my mind, my heart is lying, my soul wants to swim in purple rivers

To fall prey to other scourges.

And hop! The wandering of responsibility

That pulls me with my feet from the cloudy moon

On cold, welcoming earth. But it's warm. I'm warm.

I've become warm. Hi-hi!

I'm a warm scourge.